T0197315

Parenting a New Paradigm

Living with Awakening Children

LIGHTSONG

authorHOUSE

AuthorHouse™
1663 Liberty Drive
Bloomington, IN 47403
www.authorhouse.com
Phone: 1 (800) 839-8640

© 2016 Lightsong. All rights reserved.

*No part of this book may be reproduced, stored in
a retrieval system, or transmitted by any means
without the written permission of the author.*

Published by AuthorHouse 11/28/2016

ISBN: 978-1-5246-4929-6 (sc)
ISBN: 978-1-5246-4927-2 (hc)
ISBN: 978-1-5246-4928-9 (e)

Library of Congress Control Number: 2016918653

Print information available on the last page.

*Any people depicted in stock imagery provided
by Thinkstock are models, and such images are
being used for illustrative purposes only.
Certain stock imagery © Thinkstock.*

This book is printed on acid-free paper.

*Because of the dynamic nature of the Internet, any web
addresses or links contained in this book may have changed
since publication and may no longer be valid. The views
expressed in this work are solely those of the author and do
not necessarily reflect the views of the publisher, and the
publisher hereby disclaims any responsibility for them.*

Dedication

To my children and all the children of this world.......

Ode to my Son

wearing

only

the summer's outfit

of a little boy's dirty feet

he runs through

the mystery of the moment

accompanied

by Curious George

with laughter so powerful

it breaks down the confinement of rules

magically pirating through the seven

seas of his day

he falls asleep

innocently and absolutely certain

of his mastery of life

Before you read this book........

A call for Awakening and a Shift of Awareness is reverberating throughout our human collective consciousness. It is inviting every individual and the world civilization as a whole to accept and to actively participate in the on-going birthing of a New Paradigm of Unity Consciousness.

In the midst of worldwide chaos, violence, economic and ecological destabilization, hunger and the deepening financial inequality, there is an ever-expanding spark bursting forth within the human heart.

It is the realization and embodiment of our True Essence.

As we recognize our Essential Self, we release the ideology of separation and the hypnosis of suffering, struggling and "trying hard and never making it". This includes the need for systems. Socially and collectively, mankind established these structures to assure survival through confinement and conformity. Yet they smother creativity, authenticity, communion and sovereignty.

Children are being born fully ensouled, and have been for decades. With fire in their bellies and hearts, they do not abide by the lie of separation from our innate divinity and adherence to authoritarian structure.

It is their calling to break free from the history of mankind and to partake in the genesis of an evolutionary change of human consciousness.

However, so many of these children are traumatized; they are suffering and getting lost due to the rigidity and inability of society to meet and embrace them in their uniqueness. Instead, they are being stigmatized, medicated and pushed aside.

Parenthood and my own Awakening have inspired me to share my insights with you, trusting that we can come together in unity to invoke a vital, authentic and aware communion with our children........free of suffering and the separation from one's wholeness.

InOneHeart

Lightsong

The "Waterstate" of Children

The moment of the first breath is a powerful declaration of autonomy. It is a sacred conversion when the newborn emerges from the nurturing, protective, growth-allowing symbiosis with the mother and claims her individuality and ownership of her own life.

As parents, relatives, caregivers and society, we have to honor this initial inhalation as the beginning of the child's journey that we agreed upon to nurture, support and watch over; yet we are not its master.

Holding a baby touches deeply the heart of every person as we witness such indescribable wholeness. Oneness and purity radiate from her tiny body-the omnipotent embodiment of her inherent Divine Essence.

Every birth of a new human being is a compelling invitation to the parents, family members and the collective as a whole to heal the inner woundedness and the separateness from one's innate, essential self. It is a call to honor, sustain and promote the uniqueness of every person.

Innocent and loving, infants are living mirrors that reflect back to us the loss of unity within ourselves and the sanctity of life. Facing the inner hurt can be a very intense catharsis of ongoing healing and Awakening. However, when we answer the call, we open ourselves so profoundly to the Presence of Love within us and step out of all trauma and chaos. We remember and become again the oceanic movement of Love.

Throughout the pregnancy, newborns reside in the "water-state" of the womb to build-in unity with the mother's body and being, and the energy of the father's semen and everyday engagement-their physical bodies and to prepare for the physical birth. Arriving from this insulating shelter, the infant dwells completely in oceanic unity. Her cosmic nature manifests as the cellular rhythm of her human form, and takes command over her physical life. This fluidity is her living truth, expressing the need for nursing, touch, love and so forth. In addition, it sustains the essential vitality and maturing of the sensory system, the cellular receptors, the nervous system and digestive system.... Living and maintaining this "water-state" preserves the integrity of the child's inner oneness and fosters a deep joy, trust in and curiosity for life. It sustains an ever-expanding wellbeingness.

The cellular rhythm is the breathing awareness of our beingness on a physiological level. It is a continuous flow of oneness with oneself, life and the cosmos; a harmony that resides outside of cause and effect and purely reflects the Divine Immaculacy of Presence.

In the moment of conception an emotional, physical and spiritual/ energetic bonding is initiated between the parents and developing infant. With the physical birth of the child, this connection continues to deepen and will expand and transform its flavor throughout the life they will share. Yet, it is during the initial embrace of the newborn, when the hearts of the parents burst wide open with overwhelming love and awe that assists the "water-state" of the infant as she enters into the world of form.

So often, after the arrival of a baby and the earlier heart openings of family, caregivers and the collective, all settles back into the old status quo of life, the coping around the stress of being a parent and the emotional, intellectual and energetic upheavals caused by the stirring up of the past that a birth triggers. Instead of continuing the embrace, a pattern of withholding sets in. In some families it may occur in more subtle ways, while in others it may be more blatant. Even though parents and family still experience the feeling of love towards the child, the responsiveness of the heart is greatly restrained and diminished.

When we-as adults-hesitate to abide by the powerful impulses of our hearts to tend to the immediate needs of a child, when we give into the intellectual reasoning why we can't or shouldn't.... have an infant cradled in our arms when we sleep; keep the baby close to our body during the day, breastfeed whenever a need arises; honor the child's sensitivities and be flexible regarding how we need to do things (as only a few examples), we weaken and even stop a deep emotional, physical and spiritual bonding with our children. This causes an ongoing shock to a child's innate state of harmony, initiating a life of pain as she begins to separate from the sense-feeling knowingness of her truth in order to survive. Over time the inner wholeness governs less and less as an instinctual confusion leads to a powerful barrier of fears and insecurities, which will manifest disharmonies of many kinds throughout the child's life.

In that moment when we let the heart reign-completely and utterly unabridged-we break the wheel of hurt and the storylines of the individual, ancestral and collective past. Embracing what arises in the moment liberates our inherent awareness and we can unrestrictedly and authentically receive and reciprocate. Then, as we restore and listen to our True Presence, we become aware of the child's Essence. We enter an absolutely powerful and beautiful dance of communion, honoring and respecting one's truth and being Love in movement.

The Renaissance of
Common Sense

The relationship between parents and child originates before the physical conception. On the inner planes, as souls, a gathering occurs to contemplate a journey together for the highest benefits for all involved. It is a union in which all perfectly receive and honor each other's presence, truth, equality, interconnectedness and path.

For most individuals, this knowingness stays hidden in the recesses of their unconsciousness due to the early separation from their innate True Nature. Collectively, humanity is still mostly governed by the Ego-Mind, which organizes reality by linear reasoning without allowing space for the Great Mystery to be tangible and visible in the everyday culture of life.

Yet, this mystical communion is the very center of a flowing and expanding relationship between parents and children. It allows and furthers a coming together that is based upon being present and receiving each other from the heart in every moment.

The true nature of the heart is to dwell in and actively express One-ness. In that moment when an infant enters the physical world and our hearts burst open wide, the simplicity of Love commences its dominion. It penetrates and exposes the realities of our perceptions, the rationalization of our re-actions to one another and life and invites us to return to unrestricted openness, innocence and unity.

To love and nurture is a very immediate response of one's authentic essence. Our uniqueness thrives as we engage in the dance of interconnectedness.

Yet, due to ancient individual and collective trauma, the fear of survival constructed an entangled maze of belief structures, which maintains the impression of powerlessness, distrust of life and love and even more so the illusion that we-as human beings-are imperfect. Mankind has recycled the loop of lostness for so long by living the hypnosis that paradise is unredeemable, and therefore neglecting the truth and the movement of one's heart.

A labyrinth of complexities comes into existence and rules us when we oppress the Love and Wisdom of the Heart. Insecurities form, mental anxiety and emotional chaos reign and the need for "experts" arises because we-as a global community-have disengaged from the Path of Simplicity.

Without common sense, we spiral down into self-sabotage and destruction. The overall collective state of existence is a powerful declaration of how the ongoing loss of the inherent rhythm of beingness has turned mankind into an emotionally barbaric, environmentally destructive, technologically addicted, greedy and power hungry civilization.

Now, becoming a parent and living with children of all ages invites us to restore the Simplicity of the Heart by trusting so implicitly the bond of Love that we co-created as Divine Beings. It can blossom and expand into a shared and sustaining life of authenticity and harmony. Then, instead of reacting, we embrace...

When we observe certain mammalian animals, we witness constant physical touch and an immediate response by the adults when the young ones exhibit signs of distress. Mankind has lost this profound instinctual responsiveness towards one another and a sense of unsureness, anxiety and instability within the human psyche is the result. Mostly, the world collective is no longer at ease with life and has forgotten how to be practical and down to earth in its interactions and solution manifestations. The effect is the cry for expert opinions, time-extensive investigations, complex resolutions and ultimately more chaos.

Within every human being-regardless of age-resides the power of authority. It is an absolute life-affirming, sensible and receptive intelligence that recognizes the sacredness of the individual sovereignty and how deeply the vitality of any relationship, including family, society, etc, depends on actively expressing one's uniqueness and being in intimate communion with oneself and each other.

Common Sense is an expression of this inherent awareness. This is an inter-active movement of love, nurturance, simplicity and truth. It creates flexible structures and routines to help the child anchor into her body and life, to explore the world safely according to her capacities to learn and understand, to engage her curiosity and to create the environment that support her innate rhythm of growing physically, emotionally, mentally and spiritually.

It begins with listening deeply inside of yourself, to feel your innate core and how Love is moving you. Listen to your child from your heart and with your body. Respond and engage without your mind being in control, recognize when your past is interfering and always......

Trust your Heart, Divine

Love and your child!

The Myth of the Average Child

Within every living being-regardless of the form, density and vibration-dwells a vibrant uniqueness. It is the mystical expression of one's Divine Presence.

This individuality unfolds and blossoms by flowing according to its innate rhythm. Like a seed that contains the knowingness of how and when to grow into the plant it is supposed to be, so does a human being. There is an extraordinary intelligence and creativity in every child, fueled by the will to thrive and a never–ending curiosity to claim and engage with life in complete harmony with one's inner being.

Throughout history, the deeply layered collective and individual hypnosis of separation from the unity with the Divine (especially one's own Divine Essence) triggered an equally powerful illusion of survival, which has so destructively governed the reality and life of mankind.

Due to this very strongly ingrained perception the need for control, power and regulations arose, eradicating continuously the internal and external abilities of a person-regardless of age-to be in creative and authentic expression. Fear took over curiosity, beauty was suppressed by judgment, and ingenuity by conformity; communion was lost to survival and the capability to embrace and celebrate to struggling.

So often the need to structure one's life, to define what is acceptable and what has to be rejected is a reaction due to a core anxiety towards the unforeseeable. Life in its immense vastness and fluidity has been regarded by mankind as the enemy because of its seeming unpredictability. Loved ones die, catastrophes bring destruction; illnesses tear apart families and so forth. However, there is a profound distinction between life and reality. Life is inherently beautiful, everlasting and always giving. A reality is the sum of our perceptions, trauma and creation stories.

As an infant is born, she enters a collective reality, which does not believe in the sovereignty of a child. Instead, she is exposed to a constant array of projections, interpretations and judgments, which does not nurture the inherent rhythm of growing physically, emotionally, intellectually and spiritually.

The simple truth is that every child develops and expresses herself very differently. Similarities do not equal sameness or even predictability.

A child is perceived according to what society is able to test and measure. Charts tell us at what age our child should crawl, walk, speak, learn letters and, numbers, read, and so on. They define "normal". However, these are projections based upon what "should happen", yet they don't include nor do they focus on readiness.

Readiness signals an impulse when all the involved physical, emotional, mental and spiritual systems have reached ripeness for the next developmental engagement. Then a leap occurs that is completely in harmony with the child, and the trust in oneself continues to grow as well as the groundedness in one's body and life.

To assure the safety and continuation of a unit, whether a family or communities of different sizes and functions—like schools, workplaces, cultures, religions, societies, and so forth—a status quo is defined by laws, written rules, and the order of accepted behaviors, including manners and many more expectations, which are not always verbalized nor explained because "it's just the way it is".

Belonging is a fundamental need within the human make-up. It allows us to blossom due to the care and love we receive. Adhering to a given standard of "expected and acceptable" feeds this longing to be included. Yet it also implies the necessity to deny aspects of oneself in order to be a part of family, friends and society and therefore feel safe.

Within the regulatory body of standards lay the categories of extraordinary and ordinary. Showing signs of the first gives allowance to behavior and needs, therefore more freedom to be authentic. Nevertheless, the continuous pressure to be special undermines the ability to build and maintain a balance between giftedness and being human.

However, more and more children of all ages are exposed to a continuous increasing pressure to perform according to the expectations, unfulfilled dreams and reactions of others ... parents, teachers, friends, coaches, government, society.... it is a loop that furthers the belief "of not being enough." This dynamic causes the loss of trust in oneself and the beginning of enduring pain due to self-doubt, a sense of not belonging and the struggle of trying hard but never making it.

The uniqueness of each child is an infinite potential of intelligence, which is simply an umbrella word for wisdom, awareness, delight, authenticity, creativity, harmony, fire, passion and so on that blossoms throughout the entire life of a person.

Caring for a child starts with conception and requires the willingness to accept and respect her individuality. It is paramount to recognize that children of any age are sovereign people, whose deep longing to grow into the fulfillment of their soul and to share their joy of being with us moves them according to their innate rhythm and nature.

To create a safe environment and to nurture the blossoming of a child's true nature demands that we-as parents and as a community-revise the tendencies of habitual, unconscious routines, rules, established guidelines and definitions of how a child should be at any age. Then we allow children to develop a solid knowing of their own core and the trust to follow their hearts.

Parenting from the heart creates the space of sharing, simplicity, practicality and harmony between each member of the family as the love we feel moves us constantly.

The Sacredness of Play

We are all born with an innate curiosity to explore, create and co-create. The impulse to engage arises from our innocence. It is delight that moves us as we trustingly immerse ourselves in the discovery of ourselves and life.

An infant needs nurturance and safety to fully incarnate. Only then can her innate, cellular fluidity blossom, readying the child into authentic exploration. Becoming aware of one's fingers and toes, as an example, being able to direct them into the mouth to suck on them is a completely sensuous and juicy experience. This partakes in the inauguration of a "me" that will evolve as the baby explores and uncovers what feels good and what doesn't. At this point there is no conceptualization into "I like it" or "I don't like it," just a very instinctual, feeling-recognition of....mmh, good-safe-happy...versus...argh, unsafe-not good.

The body responds as a whole: every cell, every neuron and all the senses receive the experience. The imprinting that occurs on many levels gives information to the still maturing physical and energetic systems. On this very feeling-instinctual and formative level, play lays the foundation for self-trust, feeling safe in life, and cellular harmony.

Play is a powerful form of self-discovery and self-expression. From the very first moment when an infant begins to connect with her own body and later with her surroundings, play allows a child to deepen the unity with herself and to understand the world she resides in.

There are no goals to achieve, only the movement of constant inquiry, fueled by the awe of the mystery that is being discovered and explored. All the senses participate as the body and soul taste the vastness of life unfolding within and outside.

Imagination is the vehicle that bridges the unseen and mystical into the physical realm. Then, the realness of the imaginary touches the make-believe reality the collective is lost in. Reality is a complex tapestry of creation stories, historical conditioning, trauma-based perceptions, and survival reactivity to name a few aspects of it. This is the moment of invitation for parents-and on greater levels for the reality structure of society-to permit the permeation by the inquisitive innocence of a child to break down the walls that have imprisoned the adult world, which is barren of the palpable trueness of the cosmic beauty of every moment and being.

Playing is often contaminated by the insistence of experts of all kinds that children need to be molded into intelligent people. Their conclusion is that a child's senses have to be stimulated, starting in utero, to assure a high IQ. Stimulation is part of nurturance, yet it should not only focus on academic aptitude nor overload the sensory system. Instead, involve the wholeness of the child, her emotional and spiritual intelligence, her humanity and physical form. Otherwise, imbalances are seeded that will grow into all kinds of disharmonies throughout one's life, such as insecurities, self-doubt, anxiety and so forth.

Play supports the innate nature of a child to unfold into the realization of her knowingness. As many have already experienced and are exposed to every day, children of all ages have an understanding and awareness contained within them that just wants to be expressed and longs to expand.

Learning Is Playing.....

Playing Is Learning....

Life is an unending ocean of infinite possibilities and we are part of this exquisite, unfolding tapestry. Fostering the individual inquisitiveness of a child at any age, supports her growing capacity to pursue her interests openly with focus and fluidity.

The temperament of every child needs to be respected to avoid sensory overload, especially for infants and toddlers. A constant overload creates stress patterns. Unresolved, chronic stress mutates into emotional trauma, learning difficulties, proneness to accident and injury, as well as to probabilities of physical disease.

Playing turns into learning, simultaneously and instantaneously. Neither of them unfolds in linear fashion. When a child has accumulated whatever she needed from a certain area of play, her interest will change and she will move on. Every area of interest turns into a building block that supports the growth of a child.

Just trusting one's own knowingness of when to let go and follow one's heart is a very powerful ability that playing instills in everyone. It builds the understanding of discernment and the strength and self-assuredness to say no when the need arises.

Learning does not need to be taught. Naturally, a child absorbs what she is exploring as she plays. Playing supports the developing and maturing physiological systems, therefore leading the child to explore more complex concepts.

Most schools provide a linear approach to teaching and learning. Some children flow with it easily, others do not. School curriculums do not involve the entire sensory system nor movement of the body. They are not interest-based, but rather build upon the premise that all children have the same learning style, and that academic education has to be started at a certain age—the earlier the better. Yet when a brain is not ready to process, comprehend and integrate certain concepts, having to try to learn can traumatize a child on many levels.

The use of the color, cut out, and paste approach to engage children in learning, that starts at a pre-school age and continues far into elementary school, teaches by repetition but does not nurture curiosity or imagination. This is only one example of how so many schools focus on the litany of doing one task again and again, in the belief that kids eventually will understand. The pressure to teach a certain subject within a certain amount of time is enormous, and adds to the usage of repetition. Yet, repetition is not identical with practice. Repetitiveness mostly creates empty knowledge. In order for the hippocampus to transform temporary memories into permanent ones, a child (and this is true for adults as well) has to connect with and relate to the information and work emotionally, mentally, energetically, and even physically. Otherwise, the sensory system and brain filter out what they deem unnecessary. On the other hand, when a child inquires organically into a subject that she is interested in, all information is naturally assimilated. This supports the unique mapping of her brain and life, as well as contributing to the expansion of her soul.

Throughout the many years of their schooling, as repetition is continuously exercised, the ingenuity of children is wasted. No wonder that more and more kids cannot abide by and fit into the role of a student. Pressure and frustration builds within them due to the restraint and lack of including their self-directing inquisitiveness. To label them ADD or ADHD is an attempt to maintain the status quo of the educational system instead of realizing that change is indeed very much needed. It also violates a child's personal freedom to express her true nature. Without doing so, she cannot grow into, realize and live her innate capacities.

The simple truth is that there is no medical disorder called ADD or ADHD. The reasons for inattentiveness, time management issues, weak impulse control, and forgetfulness, to name a few of the "symptoms", are innumerous: different learning styles and needs; a weakness in the auditory or visual processing; dyslexia; a diet of too much processed food that is filled with artificial flavors, coloring and too much sugar; sleep deprivation, boredom; not being grounded in one's body; high sensitivities to the emotions and energies of others; too much stress at home....

A child's failure to adhere to the commonly prescribed standard of behavior and learning doesn't automatically mean she has a problem that requires medication.

Schools should not stifle the individuality of young people, but rather create an environment that cherishes and encourages the interests, knowingness and intelligence of their students.

Learning truly never stops. It is in our nature to stretch ourselves beyond what is familiar, in order to nurture and express our infinite essence. Playing prepares us to do so as we maintain our innocence and curiosity. Then, we become life-long explorers and co-creators of life's un-ending beauty.

Without play, life just turns into a mere existence of flatness and repeated loops as the ingenuity that dwells in every person stays hidden and awaits its awakening.

The Trouble with Vaccination

The ongoing debate about whether vaccines are safe or not is deeply rooted in polarization and fueled by recent outbreaks, fear mongering, sensationalism, misinformation and just simple greed.

It is important to understand the energetics of inoculations and the immense and open-ended impacts they have on the development and well-beingness of children throughout their entire lives.

In utero, the growing infant dwells in an ongoing symbiosis with the mother emotionally, energetically, mentally and physically. From the very moment of conception and until birth—throughout the many stages of mitosis and the stem cells differentiation that forms organs, glands and so forth—the developing body is utterly permeable and continuously absorbs. Every cell is structured according to the energetic information of the soul and the indestructible seed atoms, which contain the quintessential data from previous lives. This data is utilized to build the physical and subtle bodies. Additionally, the composition of each cell is also influenced by the state of well-beingness of both parents and their individual histories, as well as the ancestral lineage.

No mechanism of discernment has developed yet during this sacred unity. The baby has no sense of "me," no ability to be selective or perceive and create boundaries. Although the physical systems are formed at the end of the pregnancy, it will take at least two years after birth for them to develop fully. This explains the immense vulnerability of a child.

Vaccines contain aluminum (neurotoxin); mercury (highly toxic heavy metal);

formaldehyde (carcinogenic chemical); fetal diploid cell matter (human cells with DNA from aborted fetuses) live or dead viruses/bacteria and their DNA to name a few.

Knowing that a newborn dwells in one-ness with the mother and has no discriminating physiological capabilities, the inoculated serum from a vaccine is being absorbed directly into her nuclear and mitochondrial DNA.

DNA carries the unlimited potential of a person on a cellular level. It also contains the encoded, genetic information of the evolutionary history including disease patterns, emotional tendencies, mental imbalances, personal strengths and weaknesses, ancestry, ethnic origins, and so forth.

The DNA of a virus and bacterium contains the evolutionary code that enables them to utilize a host's environment for its own survival.

The genetic composition is unique in every person. It is finely calibrated and extremely fragile in children. Every gene has an on and off switch. This arrangement by which a gene is switched on or stays off is impacted by the different strains of DNA and their genetic information in the vaccines. Simply put: vaccines interfere with and change the genetic code of a child, even of an adult, because the foreign DNAs contain information and triggers that are not compatible with one's unique cellular composition and information.

Enzymes are catalysts for cellular processes. To open a specific gene segment in order to produce a certain amino acid, an enzymatic chain reaction is needed—from the moment the need is recognized by the body until the amino acid is correctly distributed. This is only one example of hundreds and hundreds of instantaneous physiological actions that take place every second in our amazing physical form. These enzyme orchestrations are like a puzzle where every piece fits perfectly in its designated space. Vaccines interrupt, disturb, disorganize, and often suppress the proper functions of enzymatic processes.

The immune system depends on the communication between beneficial bacteria, enzymes and the nervous and endocrine systems within its cellular network. Again, the substances used within the serums, do not strengthen the immune system, rather the opposite. Aluminum triggers an over-reaction of the immune system that leads to chronic inflammation. One example is the microglia of the brain and enteric nervous system. They are macrophages. Their task is to defend against harmful intruders. However, the neurotoxin Aluminum causes an excessive activity in them that leads so often to a chronic inflammation of the neural tissue.

The brain is supposedly protected by the blood-brain barrier. It is a semi-permeable membrane, guarding the central nervous system from viruses, medication and other substances. Yet, science is divided as to when this "wall" develops. Some scientists say that it is within the first trimester, others believe that it is after birth, and still others put the development around 2 years of age. Inflammation, environmental toxins, alcohol, vaccinations, drugs, ongoing stress, trauma, and auto-immune reactions all weaken the barrier in adults. For children, starting in utero, the development and functioning of the blood-brain barrier is weakened and even interfered with by vaccines and medication that the mother receives during pregnancy. It is also affected by the health history of family, and after birth, by inoculations, toxins in the environment, exposure to chemicals and so forth.

Over the years, medical science has reversed its stance on alcohol and smoking during pregnancy. Decades ago, nobody thought either of them would interfere with the development of the embryo. In October of 2015, the American Academy of Pediatrics issued the warning that no amount of alcohol is safe. Another example is the usage of antibiotics during pregnancy. Scientific evidence reveals that they influence negatively the mitochondria, the powerhouse of the cells. This is true for both the mother and baby. Statistics have shown that with the increase of vaccinations, autism, diabetes, leukemia, allergies, asthma, learning disorders and other illnesses have risen tremendously in children. Adult diseases have skyrocketed as well. The above illustrates that the blood-brain barrier does not provide absolute protection nor are the findings of medical science infallible. As with everything in life, they are a work in progress and evolving.

Because a growing child absorbs everything from the moment of conception, every decision made by parents necessitates discernment. Don't be afraid to take your time to ask questions and inform yourself. The Internet is a vast field of resources and support. There are many other disciplines, like homeopathy and natural medicine, to name only a couple, which have helped and cured people of many ailments and strengthened their well-beingness for centuries.

Falling into the fear trap is easy. Pharmaceutical companies are multi-billion dollar corporations that need to keep their stock prices up and to do so compete for a market so oversaturated with drugs that do not cure the cause of an illness but only try to alleviate the symptoms.

Be your child's fiercest advocate because true well-beingness includes every part of a person regardless her age. It is the foundation for a life of authenticity, harmony, physical health, awakenedness and creative sovereignty.

Breaking the Mold

For decades now, children have been incarnating with an activating blueprint of unity consciousness. They decided to participate in the continuous vibrational change of consciousness and physicality by breaking the mold of the collective status quo and not following their ancestral or parental lineage.

When nurtured, respected and supported in their uniqueness and truth, the simplicity of love expands continuously in a never-ending flow of harmony. When a challenge arises, with the proper support a child is able to embrace what unfolds without complex reactions or being traumatized by the situation. Therefore, no disharmonies will manifest. Then, memories are free of creation stories; without them, imprints are not established and no loops of re-occurring pain manifest.

Childhood and adolescence are times of ongoing blossoming and cellular awakening of one's true nature. Their innate divine blueprint-already present and active-physicalizes according to their own essence. Periods of intense bio-molecular and energetic changes are occurring throughout childhood and adolescence as every cell initiates a powerful metamorphosis that expands the inherent crystalline and original DNA, and sheds any remnants of the old carbon DNA structure.

If a child's true and sensitive nature is ignored, negative scripts formulate. They vary in intensity and complexity, depending on the individuality and delicateness of the soul; the circumstances and dynamics of pregnancy and birth; the family and upbringing; the cultural and social rules, to name a few examples. Anxieties; processing and learning difficulties; auto-immune patterning;

digestive problems; bonding and relating issues; problems with spatial and linear organization; frustration issues....these are all examples of the struggles that can manifest when a child has to separate from her inherent essence.

Then, especially during adolescence, a soul initiates powerful surges to break open the trauma of early childhood in order to heal. It causes an immense rawness, a sense of lostness and vulnerability as emotions and memories surface. Behavioral patterns-formed so early on-often intensify. Teenagers are extremely sensitive and defenseless during these periods of soul initiations and in great need of connecting with others and of being cared for, even if they seemingly reject all of it.

Children's brains are multi-dimensionally organized and naturally function as such, but technology should not be the only vehicle through which they relate to and engage with themselves, others and life. In order to incarnate fully into the wholeness of their essence and body, children need to be held, have all of their senses engaged and played with, follow their curiosity, explore nature, be supported and share their daily encounters with life.... An iPad should not be the babysitter nor can it create the joy and connectedness that children experience when they bake cookies with their parents.

Children of all ages need attentive and engaged parents, who provide a flexible, accepting and nurturing structure, so that a child can grow according to its innate nature, even during puberty.

Humanity is experiencing a multitude of powerful challenges. Solutions cannot be found by recreating the old. Yet, this is exactly what is happening and will continue to happen, if we-as parents, caregivers and society-continue unconscious parenting and child rearing. Then, children have to shoulder and repeat the pain and struggles of the generations before them, including those of their parents and families, instead of creating a life for themselves that radiates a new vibration of being and physicality.

It is time to be courageous in the name of all children.....so that they have a new and different future.....and the Earth as well....

My deepest and heartfelt gratitude.....

....to Susan and Allia for reading the manuscript and their honest feedback

....to Kristen for her enthusiasm and support to publish this book

....to Steve for his generous gift of editing

....to Alan, my husband, for his continuous love, support and love for adventure

....to Sven, Laura and Uleah, my children, who delight my heart beyond words

About the Author

Lightsong is a mystic, healer, writer and photographer.

For many years she has been assisting children of all ages and their families to transform physical dis-eases, emotional and mental disharmonies, and energetic imbalances. She is also a voice for those children who have none-to create a deeper understanding of who they truly are and what their needs are.

She is a gifted and passionate advocate, bringing the children's Divine future into the present.

To follow her blog, read testimonials or listen to a free meditation please go to

www.divinehealingandawakeningwithlightsong.com

Printed in the United States
By Bookmasters

Printed in the United States
By Bookmasters